The Lightworker Within. From dusk to dawn.

Taylor Murawski

BookLeaf Publishing

India | USA | UK

Presentation by *BookLeaf Publishing*

Web: www.bookleafpub.com

E-mail: info@bookleafpub.com

ISBN: 9789363309876

First edition 2024

To my inner child: This is for you. Your whole life you have been writing and waiting for this moment. Despite what everyone said, you did it!!! You wrote and published your first book, baby. All that pain finally paid off. ♥ 🙏

To my children: This is also for you. I hope that in your own hard times, you can reflect back on Mommy's words. I hope you know I'm always here, and you can also make your own dreams come true. Never give up. I love you!. Thank you for being the only ones who ever believed in me; I'll always believe in you too.

ACKNOWLEDGEMENT

I would like to thank my inner child, teen self, and adult self for these written words. We always knew one day, that we'd do something with them!. I used to always dream about writing a book, and as an adult, I finally have!. I got to visit my childhood through my words, and process them as an adult. I could feel now, what I had felt then. It was as if, I was working directly with my younger selves. I was always torn down for being a writer, and I was always told that I was not one. So this book means everything, to all versions of myself.

Thank you, to everyone who reads this!.
I hope this helps!.

Trauma Bonded.

I'll never seem to get away.
I always run back, and for awhile we're okay.
But then after awhile, it all remains the same.
It's the same two players, and the same old game.
The cycle is stuck on repeat....
And I'm starting to show, heavy defeat.
I don't know, what this is all about...
All I know, is that I need to get out.
I don't feel like I love you...
But maybe I do.
What's the explanation? Why can't I leave?
But even when I do, I'm never fully free.
I don't even know what is wrong with me...
All I can give, is a sincere apology.
The blame has always been on me.
And you always get to walk away-so perfectly.
I just wish that we were happy.
That it could go back, to how it used to be.
You open me up, just to nail me shut.
You tell me you love me, but you dgaf.
I have fallen for all of your deceit and lies.
So much so, you had control of my life.
I want to escape, but you have me trapped.
I found a way out, and it's already been mapped.
I have to break this chain attached to you.
I have to break free, no matter what I do.
The mirrors and smoke are starting to clear.
I'll stand strong, and I'll have no fear.
I'll beat this addiction created from you.

I'll get sober, no matter what I do.
I'm gonna break this cycle, and I'm gonna run...
Because this level of the game is no longer fun.

Breaking point.

You keep pushing and pushing...
Trying to see how much I can take.
Just know there will be no surprises...
When you push so hard, that I finally break.
You'll take your actions, and place them on me.
You'll always blame me, for every little thing.
My heart fills,with all this ache and all this pain.
I fill so much, that my eyes always rain.
I have all these words, and not much to say.
I have good intentions, now conquered by hate.
All I can do is pray and pray...
I'm begging God, to show me the way.
I want out of the rain, back into the sun.
I want out of this misery, back into the fun.
I'm tired of walking around with this loaded ass gun...
I'm just waiting for the shots, so I can be done.

Toxic love.

I can't get your words out of my head.
I'll never forget the things that you said.
I hold onto them closely, as I hold on tight.
Hoping one day, everything will be alright.
You swore you'd never hurt me again.
It'd never be, how it was back then.
You still have yet to show me...
You know how hard, it is for me to believe.
Don't you know, I wish you were here.
But I have looked, and you're nowhere near.
I remember the last time I talked to you.
Telling me things, that only I knew.
Sometimes, I even cry at night.
I'm just trying to win this battle, and fight.
When all I wanna do, is be with you.
Idk if I can wait, and it's killing me too.
I think about letting go, and then I hear our song...
Maybe it's God stopping me from moving on...
But I only wanna hear it from you.
No one can say, the words that you do.
I know things like this, hit you to the core.
But I honestly, just don't know anymore.
If you were around, things would be fine.
That's how it always is, between you and I.
I think this time, I have a chance to be okay...
If I truly do, ever walk away...
But that was never me....
It was never you, that I could leave...

When we're good and moving forward, we fall back...
And everything we had, is lost between the cracks...
This time, I'm leaving it on the ground....
I'm going where I'm free, and where love can be
found.

Hiding.

I didn't want to admit it.
It was easier to lie.
And to hide the emptiness...
To smile, instead of cry.
I lock away the pain, put away the fears.
I show only smiles, not the hidden tears.
I can't even get you off of my mind...
I still think about you-all of the time.
It's not so plain to see...
You're the one who does this to me.
And I hate the thoughts inside my head...
Not wanting to be alive, but not wanting to be dead.
I sit in my silence, I sit in my misery.
I write a few poems, and purge out your energy.

Help me.

Help me out of my misery.
Take all of this pain, away from me.
I don't know what I'm needing.
But I know that I'm tired of bleeding.
I can't get this out of my head.
And I'm seeing nothing, but the color red.
Please hurry, I'm in a hurry.
I don't know how I feel, emotions all blurry.
Half alive, and almost dead.
No, I'd rather not love myself instead.
Who do you think, that I really am?
I really thought, that you'd understand.
And if it helps your theory....
I am living life, in conspiracy.
I live my life in silence.
Yet inside, I feel so much violence.
I don't know what it's all about....
But I do my best, and block it out.
I'm on the cliff, and I feel like jumping.
There's a lot of fear, but my blood is still pumping.
My life isn't going anywhere....
So deep inside, I do not care.
Why must I always live like this?
Why do I get through life, cutting my wrist?
I look at all the blood trickling down...
But I only do it, when no ones around.
I've been going in for the kill....
But unfortunately, I am here still.

Fake love.

More than you know...
It's better to let this go...
I'm tired of you always hurting me.
I'm always begging you, so desperately.
You're always out here lying.
And I'm always out here crying.
I know that I've made this extremely clear.
Don't pretend, that you don't see my tears.
You listen to my words, but never ever hear.
You always bring to life, my biggest fears.
My heart is stalling....
And my mind is falling....
Maybe you're just not meant for me.
As time goes by, that's clear to see.
Look at me here, still whining....
Look at me here, still crying....
I remember the days, you were gonna die.
You were so ready, and so was I.
All you did was mess with my head...
Left me broken, and left me for dead.
My heart is so broken...
And I'm not even jokin'....
How could you even do me like that?
Turn your back, and never come back.
When all I ever did, was run to you.
I always did, whatever you wanted me to.
Unfortunately, those days are ending....
Because I'm done, sitting here pretending...
I loved you, with every line true.
I loved you, but you didn't love me too.

Trauma bond, not love.

I try to block out thoughts of you.
But thinking about you, is all I do.
When people say your name, I ask "who"?
But deep inside, we all know the truth.
Why do I lie, when there is no use?
Everyone already knows, how much I love you.
I just wanna be set free....
But you have a deep hold on me.
I move forward, and then I fall back.
But you already know, don't have to say all that.
I have to get you out of my mind.
And get you out, forever this time.
I really do just need to realize...
That this time, I will be alright.
I have to make a move...
And I have to make it, far from you.
I know it's gonna be hard to do....
But I have no choice, I know that I have to.
I can't seem to stay away from you.
It is something, I still can't do.
Through-out of all this friction....
You are still, my greatest addiction.
When it's all said and done...
You make the pain feel, as if there is none.
I just find myself, always confused...
However I guess, that's all old news.
You come close, and I push you away.
I come close, but you never stay.

Why can't we just be on the same page?
We're writing a new story, every single day.
I think you might know more than me...
It really is time, that one of us leaves.

Love poem.

If anything in my life is worth it...
It is you, baby you are perfect.
I think of you every day and night.
In your arms, everything feels alright.
When I see my reflection in your eyes....
It lets me know to hold on, and to hold on tight.
I just need you to know....
I never wanna let you go.
I know that if I ever did...
That decision would be so stupid.
I know that others have competed...
But only with you, do I feel completed.
I don't ever wanna hurt you.
Hurting you, would hurt me too.
I loved you then, and I love you now.
I wanna pick you up, not knock you down.
It took more than a few tries....
But like they say: true love never dies.
The love is strong between you and I...
So it's okay, if we break down and cry.
Is this too good to be true?
I don't even care, as long as it's with you.
You are everything to me.
No one could ever make me think differently.
They also say that love is blind...
Our vision is clear, we'll make it this time.
I am yours, and you are mine.
Together forever, in every lifetime.

Heart break.

This song brings back so many emotions...
Who knew my tears could create a real ocean.
Although, that may be a metaphor...
You know exactly, what it stands for.
I find myself often, getting carried away.
That's the whole reason, I'm writing this page....
I remember the days fighting for you.
But all you ever did, is what you wanted to.
I had every reason to open my skin...
From all the pain, that I have held within.
Sometimes, that's just what it takes.
Having to heal, from massive heart break.
Why couldn't you just wipe my tears away?
Why couldn't you just say, what I needed you to say?
The emotional trauma soars through my veins.
I let it all out, by creating red stains.
I know there must be a healthier way...
But I'm not sure, so I can't for sure say.
I'm weighed down often, by all this pain.
I can't take it anymore, driving myself insane.
I never thought it could be too late.
But now it is, and I can't think straight.

Betrayed.

All these people say, things that aren't true.
And it is your exes, who say them to you.
How do you expect me to sit back and smile?
You know shit gets to me, after awhile.
How do you expect me to keep a smile on my face?
When all I'm doing, is being replaced.
Except this time, you're the one losing me.
So I hope this all makes you happy.
I'm sick of being sucked, into this tide.
I see it all now, eyes opened wide.
I'm so broken, and I'm so torn.
I truly can't take this shit anymore.
And in all honesty, it really just seems....
That you never have the time, for only just me.
It's okay, leave me out in the dust.
Go ahead, go chase after lust.
I'm still trying to be okay....
What do you expect me to say?
All I wanna do is fall, and stay asleep.
But I cannot, because the pain is too deep.
So all I do is lie wide awake....
I'm holding it in, emotions about to break.
Even after all we've been through...
All I ever wanted, was just you.
But now that I have you back here with me...
I'm just not sure, this is where I wanna be.

Done.

Your love is a lie.
Just a waste of my time.
It's just too bad, that I didn't know.
It's just too bad, I refused to let go.
I hate how I'm the one, trying to make it work.
When I'm the only one, whose getting hurt.
I keep thinking I can change you.
But you'll only change, if you really want to.
With me not knowing what to say.
I just keep on praying, day after day.
You always talk a big game, wearing big shoes.
But you always knew, I had issues.
By following you, I was following my heart.
But all you ever did, was rip it apart.
You said you'd never hurt me again.
But it's all the same shit, I heard back then.
It is you, who hurt me too much.
So you can't blame me,for wanting to giving up.
You brought this all on yourself.
You cannot place blame on anyone else.
You seem to think this is all a game.
But I'm sorry honey, I do not play.
I'm leaving you, right where you belong.
And won't be long, before I'm really gone.

But I love you, don't know why I do.

I hate you.
And all the things you put me through.
But, I love you.
Don't know why I do.

I hate crying, to where I can't breathe.
I just wish I had, the strength to leave.
But, I love you.
Don't know why I do.

I hate how you keep lying.
I wonder why I keep trying.
But, I love you.
Don't know why I do.

I hate wondering where you are.
And wishing upon the same ol star.
But, I love you.
Don't know why I do.

I hate that I'm locked in my shell.
Beneath I'm breaking, and you can't tell.
But, I love you.
Don't know why I do.
I hate how without you, I can't live.
I hate how I accept, everything you give.
But, I love you.
Don't know why I do.

I hate how you play with my mind.
One day you hate me, the next day you're fine.
But, I love you.
Don't know why I do.

I hate how you make my skin crawl.
How without you, I'm in withdrawal.
But, I love you.
Don't know why I do.

I hate how you come and go.
I hate to know the things, no one else knows.
But, I love you.
Don't know why I do.

I hate that I write these poems for you.
I sit and wonder, why I do.
But, I love you.
Don't know why I do.

Lights out.

I guess I just don't have much to say.
Even if I did, I wouldn't say it anyways.
I know me being locked up,cuts you to the vein.
But I swear to you, I'm the best kind of stain.
I have broken dreams, and alcohol breath.
I keep pushing,and putting it to the test.
I guess I should have never been alone.
Now look at me, losing all control.
Look at my life, just spiraling down.
Look around me, ain't no one around.
In my life, there's nothing left.
In my heart, I just feel depressed.
Maybe I chose to lay in my own grave...
I wish it was me, they were trying to save.
I just need to be saved from myself.
But I can't exactly tell anyone else.
I'm hoping someone will care enough to see...
I hope that they will see,the light dying in me...
Some days are dark and blue...
But when I'm asked, I never tell the truth.
No one wants to hear my words, so I just write.
It's the only way, for my light to reignite.
I mostly hold everything, close to the chest.
I speak only a little, and then I write the rest.
One day I'll be outspoken, and I'll be free.
And you will see me, with everything I need.
My poems will go from darkness to light.
And you will know, I have won this fight.

Trigger warning.

Waking up, in the middle of the night.
Why must mommy and dad always fight?
All I can hear, is their loud screaming.
Oh no mommy, why are you bleeding?
I promise one day, I'll stop all the beatings.
I'm here to help, just grab my hand.
You'll never leave, and I don't understand.
Dad, why do you always smell like booze?
Why does mom, always have a big bruise?
When I'm older, he'll fight someone else.
He will learn, to keep his hands to himself.
This is something, we don't speak about.
But I swear one day, I'm gonna get us out.
After all these years, I still wake up.
I still know what it means, when the door is locked
shut.
I'm full of fear, but time to clear my mind.
It's happening now, gonna stop it this time.
I hear the smacks, and I hear the cries...
I'm running in, no time to think twice.
He took off, we better hide the knives.
I just want him to leave her alone...
Can't call for help, he broke all the phones.
I'm only a child, having to act grown.
When I became older, I fought back....
I kept my promise, and they never saw that.
Mommy, I broke us all free.
And for that, you'll forever hate me.
Dad, I finally got to beat you.
Just like God always told me to do.

Take it.

Take me, take it all.
Cut me open, and let me fall.
Don't let me grasp for one last breath.
Don't catch my fall, let me bleed to death.
My scars are yours to keep.
So kiss them tonight,before you go to sleep.
Pull out my threads, pull them like hair.
Pull it all out, I know you don't care.
Because right now, that's just how I feel.
No more safety pins, and covering the seals.
It's just all coming undone.
Letting go of love, as if there was none.
Looking back, there wasn't really anything.
And now all I have, are worthless memories.
You can now, tell me everything.
And now, it won't even mean a damn thing.
You cut me all the way open.
Left me here, bloody and broken.
So take me, and take it all.
Cut me open, make me crawl.
Don't let me grasp for one last breath.
Make it count, put me to death.

Lost in self.

I just sit, and I think to myself...
Thoughts only I know, and nobody else.
Even when I'm just laying in bed...
I cannot escape, these thoughts in my head.
I wonder if, it'll ever be okay...
Reminding myself, to take it day by day.
Things are hard, and then they seem easy.
The weather is cold, and then it seems breezy.
One minute happy, the next minute sad.
I keep lying to myself, that it can't be that bad.
I wonder how, I've lost all control.
There's this side of me, that I don't even know.
I always look back on the life I used to lead.
I look back on the days, where love was everything.
Falling back into darkness, falling into cracks.
Filling all the holes, with the things I once lacked.
I have fought hard, but seem to lose this fight.
I pray to God, and beg him for some light.
Only I can paint is this pretty little picture.
And wash it all down, with this bottle of liquor.
Once upon a time, I was headed in the right direction.
Until I opened up,and found my imperfections.
I'm trying to feel alive, but mostly feel dead.
And there is nothing I can do, to escape the voice in
my head.

Love lost.

I remember how in love, that we used to be.
As long as we were together, we were happy.
It never mattered the time or the place.
We always had smiles, and love on our face.
All of our friends, were rooting for us.
No one in this world, could come between our trust.
Every moment spent, a moment in heart.
Nothing in this world, could tear us apart.
Yeah things were good for a couple of months.
And then little things, started to pop up.
Some things, that would forever hurt me.
It left me so blinded, and I could not see.
Every word you said, didn't mean a thing.
But even then I couldn't set you free.
It messed me up, and I made myself sick.
And disgustingly, you helped me through it.
After while things just got too hard.
We were together, but mentally apart.
We always thought, that love would be easy.
But all it did was leave us feeling crazy.
You always had me down, begging on my knees.
Wishing and praying, that you wouldn't leave me.
All you ever do, is leave me here waiting.
I'm stuck in my head, I'm stuck here debating.
Is this where it ends, or where it begins?
We always said we'd stay, through thick and thin.

Wars within.

Yet again, I can't go to bed.
I'm too busy listening to the voices in my head.
But if I fall asleep...
Don't wake me in my dreams.
I'm almost to the point, where I don't wanna breathe.
But nobody cares, and deep inside I bleed.
If this is depression, it's spreading like disease.
I don't know what it is, but it's consuming me.
How can you past judgement, right or wrong?
How can anyone blame me for not being strong?
I sit in this darkness, and can't find the sun.
In the back of mind, there is a loaded gun.
Deep deep inside, I'm falling apart.
Slowly drifting off, with a hole in my heart.
I don't wanna have to sit,in this empty silence.
I feel nothing inside, except rage and violence.
I cannot seem to escape this so far.
I've really been trying, and trying real hard.
I no longer want to feel broken and torn.
I don't know how much more of this, I can take
anymore.
I never thought I'd be this far gone.
I wanted to tell, but I had no one.

Selfish.

Me helping you, is messing my life up too.
But you don't care, as long as I do.
You tell me to take all of these pills.
Maybe I shouldn't, but I probably will.
I do the things, I don't wanna do.
But you do things, to make me listen to you.
And even when I do say no.
You sit there and act as if I don't.
I get so messed up, that my body feels numb.
But who cares, as long as you're having fun.
You want my everything, you want my all.
But you do nothing, but ignore my calls.
You also take all of my energy.
How much do you expect me to feed?
I can't give you a home, I can't give you money.
All you want, is control of my body.
You know that I have my own issues.
But you don't care, you want the focus on you.
You always say, you're life is going to hell.
Because of you, mine is as well.
You're supposed to keep me out of trouble.
But all you ever do is make that shit double.
You think that you're some kind of thug.
You only support me, by feeding me drugs.
When I want to open up, and talk about why.
You shut me up, and all we do is get high.
It only helps for a short little while.
When it runs off, I'm a hurt inner child.
I have to escape from this abuse.
I must get sober, and get away from you.

Broken.

I remember falling down to my knees.
Begging God no, and begging God please.
How could you really not see?
Wtf, you were doing to me?
I fell down to the ground-wrist bleeding.
Pills and alcohol, and now I'm ODing.
I can't believe the things that I am seeing.
I'm holding on, but I'm barely still breathing.
I begged you not to leave me all alone.
And I was screaming so loud on the phone.
You knew it was menon the other line.
& You didn't care, as long as you were fine.
All I could do is cry, cry, and cry.
All you could do is tell your pretty little lies.
You're not who I thought, you are someone else.
I can't believe I thought, you'd save me from myself.
I can't escape the pain, I see it in my dreams.
I try to hold it in, but I let out all the screams.
You have betrayed me in the worst way.
And I blame myself, I can't believe I stayed.
You my dear, will pay for your sins.
Because in the end, God always wins.

Eggshells.

I don't know why I even try.
Because nothing makes you satisfied.
You're always mean, and you make me cry.
You always blame me, and I don't know why.
When you come home I pretend I'm asleep.
I hold my breath, and don't make a peep.
I think of how I'm gonna get away.
I think of this, all night and day.
I don't wanna leave and it be a mistake.
But staying here only makes my heart break.
And then you get mad, another hole in the wall. We
stay fighting, and the cops are being called.
How can you say "baby, I love you".
But hurt my body, and do what you do.
I try and hide all of the bruises.
But everyone knows, so it's really just useless.
I can't believe the one I fell in love with.
Is smashing things,and hitting me with fists.
Here we go, you're drinking all this beer.
Here comes the drama, here comes my fears.
You get so drunk, you can't even speak clear.
Here comes the trauma, here comes my tears.
This is the night that I have to escape.
Because if I don't, it might be too late.